PRIDE AND PREJUDICE ABRIDGED

A short comedy by
Laura Pittenger

Based on the novel by Jane Austen

www.youthplays.com
info@youthplays.com
424-703-5315

 ISBN 978-1-62088-724-0.

COPYRIGHT RULES TO REMEMBER

1. To produce this play, you must receive prior written permission from YouthPLAYS and pay the required royalty.

2. You must pay a royalty each time the play is performed in the presence of audience members outside of the cast and crew. Royalties are due whether or not admission is charged, whether or not the play is presented for profit, for charity or for educational purposes, or whether or not anyone associated with the production is being paid.

3. No changes, including cuts or additions, are permitted to the script without written prior permission from YouthPLAYS.

4. Do not copy this book or any part of it without written permission from YouthPLAYS.

5. Credit to the author and YouthPLAYS is required on all programs and other promotional items associated with this play's performance.

When you pay royalties, you are recognizing the hard work that went into creating the play and making a statement that a play is something of value. We think this is important, and we hope that everyone will do the right thing, thus allowing playwrights to generate income and continue to create wonderful new works for the stage.

Plays are owned by the playwrights who wrote them. Violating a playwright's copyright is a very serious matter and violates both United States and international copyright law. Infringement is punishable by actual damages and attorneys' fees, statutory damages of up to $150,000 per incident, and even possible criminal sanctions. **Infringement is theft. Don't do it.**

Have a question about copyright? Please contact us by email at info@youthplays.com or by phone at 424-703-5315. When in doubt, please ask.

CAST OF CHARACTERS

ELIZABETH BENNET, the middle sister.

JANE BENNET, the eldest sister.

LYDIA BENNET, the youngest sister.

MRS. BENNET, their mother.

MR. BENNET, their father.

CHARLOTTE LUCAS, their friend.

MR. COLLINS, their cousin.

MR. BINGLEY, their neighbor.

MR. DARCY, his friend.

LADY CATHERINE DE BOURGH, Mr. Darcy's aunt.

MR. WICKHAM, Mr. Darcy's sworn enemy.

MESSENGER, to the Bennet family.

SETTING

Georgian/Regency England, early 1800s.

PRODUCTION NOTES

ON CHARACTER DOUBLING: Should there only be 10 actors available, the Author suggests that the roles of Charlotte Lucas and Mr. Collins be doubled with the roles of the Messenger and Lady Catherine de Bourgh; the Author leaves the precise division of these two roles between actor and actress at the discretion of the Company.

If more than 12 actors wish to perform the play, non-speaking background roles may be added. The Company may wish to supply the Bennet family with two additional daughters (the non-speaking roles of Kitty and Mary, upon whom the original plot unfortunately does not hinge); Mr. Bingley with a pair of haughty sisters; or Mr. Darcy with a young sister. Mrs. Bennet could be supplied with friends with whom to gossip, or Lydia with English naval officers with whom to flirt. Costumed maids or footmen could be responsible for setting the scenes, helping the audience to understand where each scene takes place.

However, the Author strongly cautions the Company that despite any additional non-speaking roles that may be added to the production, absolutely no dialogue or "shadow play" are to be added to or subtracted from the play, which should be performed exactly as written, with a running time of no greater than 15 minutes. The quicker, the better.

ON TONE: This play is fast, silly, and farcical. Extravagant hats and quick, observable character-based costume changes are highly encouraged. For the budget-conscious, the Author notes that Regency dresses are as simple as tying a floor-length nightgown or bedsheet about the bust with a rope or a belt.

DEDICATION

To Dr. Joanne Edmonds: for sharing your wisdom.

To Jane: for all the rest.

(Lights rise on the entire company and focus on ELIZABETH BENNET. Note: You may wish to keep the entire company onstage for the entire play, or just waiting in the wings, in order to quicken entrances and exits.)

ELIZABETH BENNET: *(As the curtain rises:)* It is a truth universally acknowledged that—

BINGLEY: —A single man—

DARCY: —In possession of a good fortune—

ALL: Must be in want of a wife!

(At the Bennet estate. Elizabeth, MR. and MRS. BENNET, JANE and LYDIA gather.

MRS. BENNET: My dear Mr. Bennet, have you heard that Netherfield Park is lent at last?

MR. BENNET: *(Newspaper held in front of face:)* Hmm?

MRS. BENNET: A Mr. Bingley, five thousand pounds a year! What a fine thing for our girls!

MR. BENNET: Mmm.

MRS. BENNET: Oh, you simply must call on him, Mr. Bennet, for the sake of my poor nerves!

(Mr. Bennet grunts.)

Have it your way! I never want to hear of him again!

MR. BENNET: Too late, I've already called.

MRS. BENNET: Oh Mr. Bennet! My hero!

(Music plays. A dance. Entire company is gathered. In character are CHARLOTTE, MR. DARCY, MR. BINGLEY, Elizabeth, Jane and Lydia.)

JANE BENNET: Oh, look, Elizabeth! It's Mr. Bingley! Look how handsome he is. And Mr. Darcy! Worth ten thousand a year, I heard.

ELIZABETH BENNET: Oh, he certainly is handsome. His character is thereby complete!

JANE BENNET: Don't be such a cynic, Lizzy.

ELIZABETH BENNET: In this society? Are you kidding me?

LYDIA BENNET: Excuse me, I was told there would be officers at this party.

ELIZABETH BENNET: Shut it, Lydia, no one asked you to come.

BINGLEY: Would you care to dance, Miss Bennet?

(Jane nods and smiles. They dance.)

CHARLOTTE LUCAS: She's never going to reel him in if she won't even open her mouth. Worth it for that prize pig.

ELIZABETH BENNET: Charlotte Lucas, we might be poor, but in this family, we marry for love, not money.

CHARLOTTE LUCAS: You let me know how that works out for you, sweetheart. Happiness in marriage is entirely a matter of chance.

BINGLEY: Darcy, there's plenty of cute girls just standing around. Live a little! See Elizabeth Bennet? She's pretty hot.

DARCY: She is tolerable, but not handsome enough to tempt me.

ELIZABETH BENNET: What a rude, contemptible, detestable man! I wouldn't marry him if he were the last man on earth.

(At the Bennet estate. All exit except Mrs. Bennet and Jane.)

MRS. BENNET: Jane, it looks like rain! You ought to go visit Bingley. You'll get sick and have to spend the night.

JANE BENNET: Mother! That's scandalous.

MRS. BENNET: Well, not in his room. Unless it gets that far.

JANE BENNET: Fine, I'll go.

(She hacks violently. Mrs. Bennet exits.)

(At the Bingley estate. MR. Bingley enters)

BINGLEY: Jane! What are you doing here? Don't speak, just follow me into the bedroom.

(Jane does the thumbs up and exits with Mr. Bingley. Elizabeth enters looking for Jane.)

ELIZABETH BENNET: Jane! Jane! Are you all right?

(Mr. Darcy enters.)

DARCY: Miss Elizabeth.

ELIZABETH BENNET: Mr. Darcy.

DARCY: May I inquire after your health?

ELIZABETH BENNET: Pardon me, my sister's basically dying for a night with Mr. Bingley, so can you please—

(Jane and Bingley enter.)

JANE BENNET: *(Through a cold, to Elizabeth:)* I'm all better now, we can go home. I think he really likes me.

DARCY: I just wanted to inform you that—

ELIZABETH BENNET: We really must be going.

BINGLEY: Goodbye Jane! Come back soon!

DARCY: That you have the finest eyes I've ever seen.

BINGLEY/ELIZABETH: Someone's got a crush.

(Darcy and Bingley exit.)

(At the Bennet estate. The Bennet family and MR. COLLINS enter.)

MR. COLLINS: Hello, my dear Bennet cousins! My name is Mr. Collins and I have recently become a clergyman and am so fortunate as to be distinguished by the patronage of the Right Honorable Lady Catherine de Bourgh, and I would like to consider all of you as potential spouses for me before your father dies and I take the house. English law, dears. Now who's free?

(Lydia screams and runs away.)

MRS. BENNET: Well, Jane's practically engaged to Mr. Bingley, so you might consider—

(MR. WICKHAM enters.)

WICKHAM: Pardon me, ladies, I'm new in town.

LYDIA BENNET: *(Running back, gasping:)* An officer!

WICKHAM: And who might you be?

ELIZABETH BENNET: Miss Elizabeth Bennet.

WICKHAM: George Wickham. British army.

LYDIA BENNET: I like the way you've loosened your cravat.

(Elizabeth kicks her out of the way.)

WICKHAM: Such a pleasure—tell me, do you know Mr. Darcy?

ELIZABETH BENNET: That rude, contemptible—

WICKHAM/ELIZABETH: Detestable man?

ELIZABETH BENNET: The very same!

WICKHAM: He screwed me over. Owes me money, big time. We used to be childhood friends and he turned into a real turd when his father died. Wouldn't give me my inheritance.

ELIZABETH BENNET: This just increases my negative opinion of him!

WICKHAM: I encourage and share your prejudice. He is quite proud.

ELIZABETH BENNET: Are you free tonight? There's a big party.

WICKHAM: Can't, if Darcy's gonna show.

ELIZABETH BENNET: Bummer. I'll miss you.

MR. COLLINS: Save the first dance for me, Miss Elizabeth!

ELIZABETH BENNET: Oh God.

(A party. Music plays. All are gathered.)

LYDIA BENNET: What a magnificent party! So many officers with whom to flirt!

MRS. BENNET: And I want everyone here to know that we'll soon have a very wealthy daughter!

MR. COLLINS: Miss Elizabeth! You owe me a dance, Miss Elizabeth!

ELIZABETH BENNET: Would you all please just cut it out?!

DARCY: MISS ELIZABETH.

ELIZABETH BENNET: Mr. Darcy.

DARCY: Will you do me the honor of this dance?

ELIZABETH BENNET: Umm...okay.

(They dance.)

You're not very good at small talk, are you?

DARCY: I'm not good at talking to strangers.

ELIZABETH BENNET: Nor at keeping old friends.

DARCY: If you're talking about this Wickham business—

ELIZABETH BENNET: Save your breath. I've heard everything.

(Darcy, stung, exits.)

(At the Bennet estate. All exit except Bennet family.)

What a lousy party that was. And so embarrassing to my family's honor. Jane, did you talk to Mr. Bingley yet?

JANE BENNET: I almost said "hello." *(She exits.)*

MR. COLLINS: *(Entering:)* Miss Elizabeth! I've been looking for you for hours, I simply must ask you something.

ELIZABETH BENNET: WHAT?!

MR. COLLINS: First of all, I think all clergymen should get married, it sets a good example for the parish. Second, marriage would make me very happy. Third, and this is most important, Lady Catherine de Bourgh has strongly advised me to find a suitable partner. Think of your family. Your poor mother will be tragically thrust from Longbourn if I don't marry one of you. You wouldn't want that, would you?

ELIZABETH BENNET: Listen, I understand all that, but I definitely can't marry you. It would be horrible for both of us.

MR. COLLINS: It's cute the way you say no.

ELIZABETH BENNET: Well I mean it!

MRS. BENNET: Ungrateful child! I will never speak to you again!

MR. BENNET: Lizzy, your mother will never speak to you again if you marry Mr. Collins, and I will never speak to you again if you do.

ELIZABETH BENNET: Thank you, Papa—

MR. COLLINS: Suit yourself, no skin off my back.

CHARLOTTE LUCAS: *(Entering:)* Oh, Mr. Collins. I'm single.

MR. COLLINS: You'll do. What's your name again?

ELIZABETH BENNET: Charlotte! What are you doing?

CHARLOTTE LUCAS: Getting it while it's hot, honey.

(Charlotte and Mr. Collins exit.)

JANE BENNET: *(Re-entering:)* Lizzy! Lizzy! I went to London and Mr. Bingley never once came to see me! He doesn't love me!

ELIZABETH BENNET: Don't be silly, of course he does! But why wouldn't he visit? Unless...

(Darcy enters, all scatter except Elizabeth.)

DARCY: Miss Elizabeth. In vain I have struggled. My feelings will not be repressed. You must allow me to tell you how ardently I admire and love you.

ELIZABETH BENNET: Uh.

DARCY: I know your family's lower in rank than mine, and I'm dating down a bit, but I love you and I want to marry you.

ELIZABETH BENNET: Well, I'm sorry you feel that way.

DARCY: Why are you rejecting me?

ELIZABETH BENNET: Did you just hear yourself? And you split up my sister and Mr. Bingley, didn't you?

DARCY: She doesn't like him! She won't even talk to him!

ELIZABETH BENNET: And what about Mr. Wickham?

DARCY: That turd got what he deserved. So that's it then? That's a no?

ELIZABETH BENNET: Clearly. You know what? I don't even care if I hurt you. Maybe I would care if you had behaved in a more gentleman-like manner.

DARCY: Read this letter, it explains everything.

(He exits. Elizabeth reads.)

ELIZABETH BENNET: "Listen, I'm sorry for ruining Jane's life. I really thought her perpetual silence meant she didn't care about my best friend and I couldn't have that. Also, Wickham's a scoundrel who blew all his inheritance money from my dad on gambling and loose women. Then he tried to kidnap and sleep with my little sister. So yeah, I hate the guy. Sorry I couldn't be more eloquent about this in person, because it would have saved us a lot of time. Yours, Darcy. P.S. Pemberley is free for tour groups." I'll have to check that out.

(She does.)

(At the Pemberley estate.)

Wait a minute, I passed up this!? Gee, maybe he's not such a bad guy after all. This house is huge! And the gardens! He's loaded! I wouldn't mind being mistress of all this.

(Darcy enters.)

DARCY: Miss Elizabeth.

ELIZABETH BENNET: Mr. Darcy! I didn't know you'd be here.

DARCY: I live here.

ELIZABETH BENNET: Right. Well, it's very pretty.

DARCY: Thank you. Would you like to come and have some tea with my perfect sister and me?

(A MESSENGER enters with a letter for Elizabeth. She takes it. Messenger exit.)

ELIZABETH BENNET: *(Reading the letter:)* What's this? "Dear Lizzy, my former favorite daughter Lydia has run off with Wickham and disappeared in London. We are all ruined. Good luck snagging a husband now. Love, Mama." I must away to Longbourn, my family needs me!

DARCY: Please come and have a cup of tea, you look frazzled.

ELIZABETH BENNET: I really need to get home.

DARCY: Don't worry. I've got your back.

(Darcy exits.)

(At the Bennet estate. Mrs. Bennet, Jane and Elizabeth onstage.)

MRS. BENNET: Oh Lizzy! My nerves, my poor nerves! Lydia has ruined us all!

JANE BENNET: We've missed you! We are all in an uproar! Papa has gone to London with our uncle to try and find them.

(The same Messenger enters with a letter.)

ELIZABETH BENNET: "Dear Lizzy, we have found Lydia and Wickham. They're not married, but we're going to force them, for a nominal fee of...a lot of money. Don't know where it's coming from, but we seriously owe your uncle for footing the bill. Love, Papa."

MR. BENNET: *(Entering, out of breath:)* Postal service travels fast these days. This is all my fault. I shouldn't have let her out of the house. I was too indulgent.

ELIZABETH BENNET: Don't beat yourself up, Papa! Jane and I are so well-adjusted it's only natural you should forget the rest of your five daughters.

MR. BENNET: *(Looking around in dismay:)* Wait—FIVE!?

(He may spend the rest of the play looking for the others, as though he had misplaced them at some point.)

LYDIA BENNET: *(Entering, Wickham in tow:)* Haven't I caught myself a handsome officer husband, everybody?

MRS. BENNET: Oh, my darling Lydia! You're the most precious of them all! One daughter married!

WICKHAM: Sorry, Miss Elizabeth.

ELIZABETH BENNET: Just make sure you don't gamble all your Lydia prize money away. I know what you did.

WICKHAM: Of...of course.

JANE BENNET: I'm glad that was resolved so easily.

LYDIA BENNET: You have Mr. Darcy to thank for that—oops! I wasn't supposed to say anything!

ELIZABETH BENNET: Mr. Darcy was behind this?

JANE BENNET: What on earth would he care?

ELIZABETH BENNET: Oh, Jane, you are SO behind on my life right now.

(Darcy and Bingley enter.)

MRS. BENNET: Girls, girls! The two rich men are back! Hang on to your bonnets!

BINGLEY: May I speak to Miss Bennet?

ELIZABETH BENNET: You can try.

BINGLEY: Jane Bennet, I love you. Will you consent to accept my hand in marriage?

MRS. BENNET: Jane!

ELIZABETH BENNET: Jane, come on, say something!

JANE BENNET: I... Yes! I will marry you!

BINGLEY: The sound of your voice warms my heart!

MRS. BENNET: Two daughters married!

(LADY CATHERINE enters in a rage.)

LADY CATHERINE: JUST A MOMENT! Elizabeth Bennet!

ELIZABETH BENNET: Lady Catherine de Bourgh? What are you doing here?

LADY CATHERINE: Tell me once and for all, Miss Bennet, are you engaged to my nephew, Mr. Darcy? It is impossible that such an arrangement could exist. Does it?

ELIZABETH BENNET: Not if your ladyship declares it to be impossible.

LADY CATHERINE: Impertinent, obstinate, headstrong girl! My nephew is promised to my sickly young daughter! He would never marry the likes of you! You are a disgrace to all good society!

ELIZABETH BENNET: Please get out of my house.

LADY CATHERINE: I will not go quietly! I am Lady Catherine de Bourgh, patroness of Mr. Collins! I have land and rank (and a very large hat)! You will not oppose me!

(She is dragged offstage by all available characters.)

DARCY: Miss Elizabeth, I know I've been a real turd. If your feelings are still what they were last April, please tell me so at once. My affections and wishes are unchanged, but one word from you will silence me on this subject forever.

ELIZABETH BENNET: My feelings are quite different.

DARCY: Oh. Fantastic. Well. I have worked on my small talk, if that's any consolation.

ELIZABETH BENNET: Can you repeat that thing you said before, about how ardently you admire and love me?

DARCY: Gladly, Miss Elizabeth. Gladly.

MRS. BENNET: Three daughters married! Oh happy, happy day!

(Wedding march plays. Tableau. Curtain falls. End of play.)

The Author Speaks

What inspired you to write this play?

I picked up my first Jane Austen novel, *Emma,* in elementary school, struggled through it, and barely understood a word. Fortunately, I didn't give up, and moved on to *Pride and Prejudice* in high school—and never looked back. I have been a Jane Austen fanatic ever since—I own several spinoff novels and two film adaptations, and I gobble up as many available Austenian artifacts as I can. I took a course on all six of Austen's major novels in college, and at the end of the semester, the brilliant Dr. Joanne Edmonds asked us to design a creative final project. I couldn't resist putting my own theatrical spin on this classic, and so ***Pride and Prejudice Abridged*** was born.

Was the structure or other elements of the play influenced by any other work?

I'm a huge fan of farces—***Noises Off*** is one of the all-time greats. I love watching physical comedy, quick costume changes, witty dialogue, the works. So I liked the idea of taking some of those principles of high comedy—such as you might find in the plays of Oscar Wilde—and applying them to an old classic, with some degree of irreverence. In the opinion of many experts, Jane Austen's narrator voice is far more satirical than has been portrayed in various movie adaptations of her work - some of which I am a big fan. I like to think that she would take some delight in the fact that this condensed version is a commentary on the silliness of the characters and plots of *Pride and Prejudice,* as well as a loving tribute to the book, which occasionally operates as a romantic comedy. The story is simply not a pure romantic drama!

Have you dealt with the same theme in other works that you have written?
I write about love triangles all the time, but I have not written many adaptations, nor have I written much farce or high comedy. I typically write dark comedies, often with a bit of romantic drama, and so this was a fun departure from my usual style. I think that Jane Austen's approach towards her characters follows me wherever I go, though—satirical yet gentle, acerbic yet generous.

What writers have had the most profound effect on your style?
In this particular work, influences are clearly Oscar Wilde, Noel Coward, Michael Frayn, David Ives, and of course—Jane Austen herself. Beyond this play, influences range from novelist Jhumpa Lahiri to Agatha Christie to Anne Lamott; playwriting influences are Annie Baker, Sarah Ruhl, Chekhov. I value brutal honesty, handled with grace and humor, and I value wit and wisdom.

What do you hope to achieve with this work?
I hope that both the actors and audiences see how mischievous and delightful Jane Austen's writing is, at its heart, and that they walk away with a renewed interest in diving into her work, which is still as relevant and timeless as ever. I also hope they laugh themselves out of their chairs. Either one of those achievements would make me proud. I think that people are afraid to dig into classic literature because of bad experiences in school—I'd like for people to realize that the classics can be a lot of fun.

What were the biggest challenges involved in the writing of this play?
As with any adaptation, the question is always: "What can I get away with cutting?" If you cut too much, you risk sacrificing iconic parts of the story, some of which might be

audience favorites. If you keep everything, you wind up with a five-hour BBC miniseries, and we already have a perfectly good one starring Colin Firth. When writing the play, I had to stay clearheaded about the structure of the novel and cut anything that did not serve the main plotlines—the A story, of Elizabeth and Darcy, everybody's favorite couple; the B story, of Jane and Bingley, which sets the whole novel in motion; and the C story, of the antagonist Wickham and his ill-fated intrusions into the lives of the Bennet and Darcy families. Fans of the novel will miss sisters Mary, Kitty, and Georgiana, as well as some wonderfully wicked moments with Lady Catherine de Bourgh, but I think they will find that the core of the story holds up without them. For a play that runs 15 minutes or less, sacrifices had to be made!

What are the most common mistakes that occur in productions of your work?

With my plays, I try to give the actor as much information in the text as I possibly can. It is up to the actor to give the script a close reading to find directions he or she can take in order to "find" the character. Sometimes actors don't do their homework! The easiest way to do your homework is to talk about the character with the director or a trusted friend, or to do some journaling about the character's wants and needs, based on what's already in the text. You don't need to make up any extra details about your character, and you don't have to be a good writer yourself—just look for clues in the script, like a detective, that show you where to go. If you really want to go the extra mile, I suggest reading the book, or watching a film adaptation, of which there are several. However, try not to imitate what you see other actors doing—always go back to the script and make your own choices!

What inspired you to become a playwright?

My mother claims I wrote my first puppet show at age five, so it's clear that I've needed to tell stories ever since I learned to read and thought to myself, "I want to do that." One of my first experiences of an adapted book-to-play was a traveling production of ***Around the World in 80 Days***, which remains one of my favorite novels to this day. As a quiet first-grader, I was astounded by the world the actors created with only a few sheets of backdrops, a few costumes and some props—they created the entire world and took me along with them. I never got it out of my head. If I can create that magic for somebody else, I will consider that to be mission accomplished.

How did you research the subject?
Dr. Edmonds, who taught a Jane Austen seminar at Ball State University, is a member of the Jane Austen Society of North America, and she is an excellent professor. She encouraged me to think more critically about Austen's writings, and for that I am grateful. It was easy to maintain a surface-level appreciation of Jane Austen, but to truly understand her world, further study was absolutely necessary. While I don't know if the nitty-gritty details of history I learned in class are present in this adaptation, I think that understanding the structure of the novel was most important for me as a playwright in order to adapt the novel successfully—and I've spent years thinking about *Pride and Prejudice*!

Are any characters modeled after real life or historical figures?
Jennifer Ehle and Colin Firth will always be the quintessential Elizabeth and Darcy to me, but my portrayal of the characters is faithful, at all times, to what was presented originally in the novel—if not in the way the characters speak, then in the spirit of what was said. I enjoy silly YouTube videos of kids explaining the plots to various movies and books, and at times, what the characters say in ***Pride and Prejudice Abridged*** is my "kid on YouTube explaining a movie" version of a

monologue from the novel that was originally quite eloquent. (Sorry, Jane!)

What is your writing process?
I tend to work pretty quickly once I have a fully-formed idea. I will take an evening or a weekend to flesh out a first draft of a piece, let it sit for awhile, send it to a couple of trusted friends for advice, and then attack it again with small adjustments. I will sometimes do an "exploratory draft" or write scenes which don't make the final cut in order to ascertain my characters' motivations, fears and dreams. If, however, I am writing an adaptation or something which must have a tight plot structure, I create a detailed outline before I even start writing, because there are points I know must be hit in order for the story to work, or foreshadowing that must be inserted at key moments in the story. Structure is incredibly important for plays, and if attention is paid to structure, the play runs like a self-driving car—you, as an audience member, can enjoy going for a drive without worrying or even thinking about how the car's mechanics are designed, trusting instead that it will take you safely to your destination—even if you don't quite know where you are headed.

Shakespeare gave advice to the players in *Hamlet;* if you could give advice to your cast what would it be?
I would give roughly the same advice that Shakespeare gave—speak clearly! And quickly. You are delivering a lot of plot exposition to an audience that may not be familiar with the original story. If even one line goes unheard, they'll be saying "Huh?" and won't be able to follow what comes next, or why. So be quick, confident, and lively, but above all, clear. Keep up the pace, and don't let the piece drag with too much emotion, effort, or meaning.

Also, don't try to be funny—figure out what your character

wants the most, and concentrate, with all your energy, on that one thing. For instance, Mr. Collins wants to marry a woman—any available woman. Think about what that might look like onstage. Lydia wants to find a cute officer. Mrs. Bennet wants husbands for her daughters. Mr. Bennet just wants to read his paper. These are very clear desires, and since this is a short comedy, the characters' motives don't have to be any more complicated than that!

Being funny is my job. If you trust what's in the text and play the objectives honestly, you'll get the laughs you're after.

About the Author

Laura Pittenger is an NYC-based playwright, director, and dramaturg. Her work has been seen at FringeNYC, The Playwrights' Center, 3V Theater, GI60 at Brooklyn College, The Sheen Center, The Last Frontier Theatre Conference, the Kennedy Center American College Theater Festival and Ball State University (BSU). Her play ***The Gospel of Huxley*** is published in the Smith & Kraus anthology *100 Five-Minute Plays for Study and Performance*, while ***The HVAC Plays (Or, Adventures in Living Without Basic Necessities, Like Heat and Air Conditioning)*** (FringeNYC) is available on Indie Theatre Now. In NYC, Laura has directed at Athena Theatre, Turn to Flesh Productions, The Tank and Project Y, as well as at BSU. She is a member of the Dramatists Guild and the New Play Exchange. Laura is a proud graduate of BSU and a Midwestern native. www.laurapittenger.com.

About YouthPLAYS

YouthPLAYS (www.youthplays.com) is a publisher of award-winning professional dramatists and talented new discoveries, each with an original theatrical voice, and all dedicated to expanding the vocabulary of theatre for young actors and audiences. On our website you'll find one-act and full-length plays and musicals for teen and pre-teen (and even college) actors, as well as duets and monologues for competition. Many of our authors' works have been widely produced at high schools and middle schools, youth theatres and other TYA companies, both amateur and professional, as well as at elementary schools, camps, churches and other institutions serving young audiences and/or actors worldwide. Most are intended for performance by young people, while some are intended for adult actors performing for young audiences.

YouthPLAYS was co-founded by professional playwrights Jonathan Dorf and Ed Shockley. It began merely as an additional outlet to market their own works, which included a substantial body of award-winning published and unpublished plays and musicals. Those interested in their published plays were directed to the respective publishers' websites, and unpublished plays were made available in electronic form. But when they saw the desperate need for material for young actors and audiences—coupled with their experience that numerous quality plays for young people weren't finding a home—they made the decision to represent the work of other playwrights as well. Dozens and dozens of authors are now members of the YouthPLAYS family, with scripts available both electronically and in traditional acting editions. We continue to grow as we look for exciting and challenging plays and musicals for young actors and audiences.

About ProduceaPlay.com

Let's put up a play! Great idea! But producing a play takes time, energy and knowledge. While finding the necessary time and energy is up to you, ProduceaPlay.com is a website designed to assist you with that third element: knowledge.

Created by YouthPLAYS' co-founders, Jonathan Dorf and Ed Shockley, ProduceaPlay.com serves as a resource for producers at all levels as it addresses the many facets of production. As Dorf and Shockley speak from their years of experience (as playwrights, producers, directors and more), they are joined by a group of award-winning theatre professionals and experienced teachers from the world of academic theatre, all making their expertise available for free in the hope of helping this and future generations of producers, whether it's at the school or university level, or in community or professional theatres.

The site is organized into a series of major topics, each of which has its own page that delves into the subject in detail, offering suggestions and links for further information. For example, Publicity covers everything from Publicizing Auditions to How to Use Social Media to Posters to whether it's worth hiring a publicist. Casting details Where to Find the Actors, How to Evaluate a Resume, Callbacks and even Dealing with Problem Actors. You'll find guidance on your Production Timeline, The Theater Space, Picking a Play, Budget, Contracts, Rehearsing the Play, The Program, House Management, Backstage, and many other important subjects.

The site is constantly under construction, so visit often for the latest insights on play producing, and let it help make your play production dreams a reality.

More from YouthPLAYS

ShakeSPLOSION!!! by Andrew Geha

Comedy. 75-85 minutes. 9-21+ females, 4-14+ males (14-100+ performers possible).

A madcap sprint through every play written by the Bard. From 235 years of English kings in the History Plays, to (nearly) every bloody death in the Tragedies, to every girl who dressed up as a boy in the Comedies, it's like watching Shakespeare's entire canon fired out of a cannon—scattering prose, verse and characters across the stage. Sword fights! Word fights! Witches, ghosts and murder! In 80 minutes!! Performed by teens!!!

Girls on the Brink by Rex McGregor

Dramedy. 70-80 minutes. 4-23 females, 0-8 males (4-23 performers possible).

A collection of short plays about coming of age and the dramatic impact of sudden change on young lives. From a new take on ***Romeo and Juliet*** to an Afghan girl whose days as a boy are at an end to a futuristic tale of living forever, these seven very different plays all explore that precarious moment when young people find themselves on the brink of life.

Know Your Role by Brandi Owensby

Dramedy. 40-50 minutes (flexible). 5-25 females, 5-25 males (5-50 performers possible.)

No sooner do we leave the womb than we're bombarded by society's expectations about gender. If you're a boy, you're like this. If you're a girl, you're like that. Whether it's how they dress, the rules of dating, body image, parental pressures or a host of other ways, through scenes and monologues that range from hilarious to heartbreaking, the teens of this flexible ensemble reveal how gender expectations affect them and how they "role."

The Goodcheer Home for Broken Hearts by James Grob

Comic Melodrama. 95-105 minutes. 7-30+ females, 4-30+ males (14-40+ performers possible).

Audiences get to boo, hiss, cheer and sigh in this spoof of the classic American melodrama. As the villainous Severus C. Snackwell takes aim at the Goodcheer Home for Broken Hearts, the sweet and matronly Charity Goodcheer, the smart, beautiful and great smelling Shasta Bellflower and indeed the entire backwater town of Wetwater, can the strong and sincere but soft-witted Steele Manly stop his nefarious plot?

La Bella Cinderella by Claudia Haas

Comedy. 50-60 minutes. 3-4 females, 2-3 males (6 performers total, plus optional extras).

The Primo Pasta Players turn the Cinderella tale topsy-turvy with their own brand of zany, pasta-loving fun. Help the Players get ready for the ball, save our heroine from a wild boar, and stop the villainous clown from stealing the crown. There are opportunities to add music and dance, and in the end, silly rules the land!

Kim Arthur and the Nerds of the Round Table by Daniel Guyton

Comedy. 35-45 minutes. 6-10 females, 3-7 males (10-13+ performers possible).

When the mysterious "Motherboard in the Stone" appears at Kim Arthur's favorite arcade, she and her magical friend Marlene investigate. Soon Kim realizes that only she has the power to remove the Motherboard from the Stone, thus becoming queen of Game-A-Lot. But uneasy is the head that wears the crown, and it's up to Kim to save the arcade from closing—by creating the greatest video game of all time. To do it, she'll need the help of her fellow nerds. And so begins the legend of Kim Arthur and the Nerds of the Round Table.

The Coloring Book by Bradley Walton
Dramedy. 55-65 minutes. 8-14+ performers, gender-flexible.

Animals in a coloring book are thrilled when a little boy begins to embellish them with crazy colors and off-the-wall flourishes. But when the boy's older sister begins coloring other pages in more lifelike hues, social divisions begin to form and friendships are challenged. Will existence as they know it break down? The exuberance and wonder of a picture book meet *Animal Farm* in this play offering thoughtful entertainment for performers and audiences of all ages.

Youth on the Roof by Laura King
Performable Collection. 55-65 minutes. 3-14 females, 1-9 males (4-16 performers possible).

It's the end of high school, and on the rooftops of schools, apartments, garages and more, the teenagers in these six plays are literally and figuratively standing on the edge of the precipice. Whether it's choosing whether to stay home or venture into the unknown, finding the courage to persevere in the face of failure, or asking themselves if they are truly becoming who they want to be, confronting their futures and that first step into adulthood will require a leap of faith.

Xtigone by Nambi E. Kelley
Drama. 90-100 minutes. 5-15+ females, 4-15+ males (9-30+ performers possible).

Chicago. Present day. Xtigone's brothers have been killed in drive-by shootings by each other's rival gang. Her powerful uncle calls for the bodies to be buried instead of uncovering the violence in the city streets. In this re-imagining of Sophocles' ***Antigone*** that uses poetry, dance and dialogue that speak with an urban voice, will Xtigone go against his edict and risk death in her quest for her community's truth?

40495327R00018

Printed in Poland
by Amazon Fulfillment
Poland Sp. z o.o., Wrocław